LETTERS FROM ALMIGHTY GOD

DEBORAH L. CLARK

Copyright © 2020 Deborah L. Clark

All rights reserved.

ISBN: **9798668579303**

DEDICATION

For Whitney,
My cousin, god sister, and my very best friend.

Thank you for always being there for me. You are truly an expression of God's love for me.

CONTENTS

    Introduction
    Forward
    Preface

1	Look Into The Mirror	5
2	Living Like A Kings Kid	8
3	Don't Doubt Who You Are	11
4	I Am In You	14
5	How You Pray Does Matter	17
6	I Have Decided The Outcome	20
7	Keeping A Firm Grip	23
8	My Promise	26
9	Rejoice And Be Glad	29
10	The Holy Road	32
11	Time Is On Your Side	35
12	Walk In The Light	38
13	Come To Me	41
14	Watch Your Mouth	44
15	Praise Is Your Breakthrough	47
	Bonus Content	
B1	My Grace Is Sufficient	51
B2	Your Slate Has Been Wiped Clean	54
B3	My Love For You Is Inexhaustible	57
B4	Your Future Is As Bright As Your Faith	60

    Acknowledgements

But you are the ones chosen by God, chosen for the high calling of priestly work, chosen to be a holy people, God's instruments to do his work and speak out for him, to tell others of the night-and-day difference he made for you -- from nothing to something, from rejected to accepted.

1 Peter 2:9-10 The Message (MSG)

INTRODUCTION

It is my honor and my privilege to introduce to you Deborah L. Clark and Letters From Almighty God. Letters From Almighty God is a series of messages sent by God to you, the Christian believer.

Letters have been used over the years to do many things; they are used to inform and to inspire, to encourage, elevate, and illuminate. Letters are used for correction, direction, and motivation. No matter where you are in your journey, the effects of a letter can be long lasting and serve to bring hope in the midst of despair.

Deborah L. Clark is a woman sent by God with letters that have been written just for you. These letters will accomplish many of the aforementioned purposes as letters do. However, the power that these letters possess is the power of change that rearranges your situation, leaving you not ever the same.

The promise that Letters From Almighty God, which Deborah L. Clark is offering you, is that if you will hear these letters with your heart and began to do what they're telling you to do, you will soon see that God and his word are one, and where the word of the Lord is the spirit of the Lord dwells, and where the spirit of the Lord is there is liberty, freedom, and victory.

Please tune in with your heart to Letters From Almighty God with Deborah L. Clark.

Shawn Matthew Cook
Minister, Author, and Prayer Coach

FORWARD

Many years ago, I was called by God to become a distribution center. Little did I know that I would be distributing Love Letters from God to people across the globe.

God began to speak to me daily and I was inspired by the Holy Spirit to search the scriptures and transcribe His words into letters. Initially, I thought these letters were solely for me, but I quickly realized they were meant for others as well. As I shared them, not only did they change my life, but others were encouraged, uplifted, and received hope in the midst of despair.

Every word as written in Letters from Almighty God is prophetic and can be confirmed through the holy scriptures. God expressed to me that these letters will be used to inform, inspire, encourage, elevate and illuminate His people. These letters are also intended for correction, direction, and motivation.

No matter where you are in your journey with Christ, I am confident that these letters contain the power to change and overcome any situation. God promises that if you listen with your heart and begin to do what He says, you will soon see that God and His Word are one…and where the Word is, so is the Spirit of the Lord.

Since I began writing in June 2010, I have shared these letters with numerous groups and blessed with requests to read them at many speaking engagements. I have accepted several invitations to read His letters directly to pastors and church leaders and share them on prayer lines on a weekly basis. God assured me that these letters will minister to millions; that He has a message for the Nations and I am one of the vessels He is using to demonstrate His love for all of humanity.

There is no coincidence that my name is Deborah. We learn in the book of Judges, that the prophetess had a remarkable relationship with God; to hear God's voice and share God's Word with others. Like the prophetess Deborah, my insight and confidence in Him has given me a unique position to inspire God's people. My purpose is to be led by God and to avail myself by His Word to others.

Deborah, the prophetess, accomplished great things because she was willing to be led by God and so am I.

Deborah L. Clark

PREFACE

The fact that you are reading this message at this moment in time should serve as a clear indication that your life's journey has meaning and purpose.

To assist you on this journey, God sent Deborah L. Clark, who by the power of the Holy Spirit, has written love letters just for you. Letters have been used over centuries to do many things. Letters are to remind us that he chose us to be His very own, joining us to himself even before he laid the foundation of the universe. Because of his great love, he ordained us so that we would be holy in his eyes with an unstained innocence.

As you meditate on his love for you, I pray that God will open your heart to see his truth, flooding you with light until you experience the full revelation of his love.

Please enjoy Letters From Almighty God with Deborah L. Clark and may your soul be refreshed.

LOOK INTO THE MIRROR

Dearly Beloved,

I love you with all of my heart and I want you to live a life far better than you have experienced thus far. A life that consists of joy and peace. A life that would make you the envy of all those around you. A life that would draw others to want to know me.

If you examine the scriptures on a daily basis, they, the scriptures, will cause you to become a true believer. Each and every time you need something from me, you will not allow doubt or unbelief to keep you from receiving whatever it is that you believe.

I want you to maintain a level of consistency concerning what you hear. Do not be wishy-washy and change what you believe based on how difficult it may seem to achieve. I never said that everything would come easy, but I did say that you would experience peace in the midst of waiting.

Oftentimes, it is your moral character that will keep you from living a life of perpetual expectation. Believing right is an essential component to keeping your focus on the things that concern my Kingdom. You should be living a life that differentiates your intentions, decisions, and actions from those that are in the world.

There are codes of conduct that should distinguish you from the unsaved. When your name is mentioned, it should be associated with integrity, courage, fortitude, honesty, and loyalty. When you rely on me, depend on me and have confidence in me, I will step in and do for you all that you require. People will see that you are a person of strength-- brave and capable. You do not have to worry about a thing. When you do your part, I will do my part as a responsible Father. I will never allow you to be left feeling shortchanged. Quite the contrary, you will not be able to round up enough containers to hold everything that I would generously pour into your life through my Holy Spirit.

Continue to shout and praise me, even when you are hemmed up in trouble. Troubles can develop passionate patience in you and patience in turn, forges the tempered steel of virtue, keeping you alert for whatever I will do next. You are my chosen, my treasured possession. You have been handpicked by me.

You are purified, holy, and well loved. You belong to me. As my child, you were born again with my characteristics.

Look in the mirror and if you do not see me, then that is not you. You are created in my image and in my likeness, tender hearted and full of mercy, gentle and patient, which is tireless, longsuffering with the power to endure whatever comes your way and with a good temper. You have been made righteous and everything that comes with it belongs to you.

Be mindful of what you do and say today. Let it be representative of your Lord and Savior, Jesus Christ. Do not allow your good character to be corrupted by bad company. Conduct yourself in a manner worthy of the gospel. I'm counting on you.

Love always,

Dad

LIVING LIKE A KING'S KID

Dearly Beloved,

I love you and I always want the best for you. I want you to start living like a King's kid. Jesus knew his position as my Son, and you are no different. It is important that you know your position and stay in it. I have personally placed you in a position of power, yet you keep giving it up to Satan.

It is your attitude that concerns me most. Your attitude is generally a positive or negative view of yourself. I told you yesterday that when you look in the mirror and you do not see me, then that is not you. Get a vision of who you are. Do not let your thoughts or anyone else tell you who you are. I had you in mind long before I laid down the Earth's foundation. I made you whole and holy by my love. I have blessed you in Christ with every spiritual blessing in the heavenly realm.

You no longer have to live under a continuous low-lying black cloud. A new power is an operation. The Spirit of life in Christ, like a strong wind, has magnificently cleared the air, freeing you from the law of sin and death. You do not need a telescope, a microscope, or horoscope to see that you are seated with Christ, who knew no sin, so that you would be made the righteousness of God. You are no longer a mere human being. I want you to get that in your heart once and for all and by my authority, I have extended all power and authority over to you.

As you read what I have written to you today, you will be able to see for yourself the mystery of Christ. The mystery is that people who have never heard of me and those who have heard of me all their lives stand on the same ground. They get the same offer, same help, and the same promises in Christ Jesus, but you have decided to take up my offer and follow me. Since you made that decision, you may as well take full advantage of who you are.

My plan for you is for you to live a life larger than you can imagine. I am a limitless God and there is no limit to what you can ask of me. I am the one who will rebuild you. My job is to heal the brokenhearted and to bandage your wounds. There is no limit to what I would do for you.

Remember, I am the one who counts the stars and assigns each one a name. In my greatness, I have limitless strength and I have made this strength available to you. Just get in position. My power will work in you to transform you. Just stay in position because you have been made complete in me. You are equipped for life and satisfied in me. Remember that your position is your attitude. Do not be afraid to take some risks, I will guide you. I want you to give more generously, and I will supply. Love more freely, and I will energize. Think and do more often, and I will amaze you. My spirit is deeply and gently within you.

I love you,

your Dad

DON'T DOUBT WHO YOU ARE

Dearly Beloved,

I cannot and I will not start the day without letting you know how much I love you. My unfailing love for you has never been an issue for me, so I do not want it to be an issue for you. I want you to have the mind of Christ.

You still have not fully accepted who you are. Just as you have hope and faith in me, I have hope and faith in you. I fully expect that you will take your rightful place. I fully expect that you will soon begin to operate in the fullness and the power as a child of the Highest. If I am the Most High, who do you think that makes you? I am King of Kings and Lord of Lords. That makes you royalty. There are privileges that come with coming from a family that rule the universe. It is time that you take full responsibility and take your rightful position while you are here on the earth.

You are my righteous, and you have a blood-bought right to live a life that is fit for a king. I want you to quit dabbling in sin/unbelief. It is time that you purify your inner life. Stop playing the field. Get serious about my plan for your life. Submit yourself to me and resist the devil, and he will flee from you. This is what is holding you back. Do not let your mind be led astray from pure and sincere devotion to me. Watch out for the snake that seduced Eve with his smooth patter. Do not be lured away from the simple purity of your love for me.

I need you as much as you need me. That is why my Son died for you so that you could have a relationship with me. When your earthly parents decided to have you, as humans they can only produce human life. But I wanted more for you. I wanted you to be born from above to be able to enter my Kingdom. You have been formed by my Spirit. You cannot see it or touch it. My Spirit is like the wind. You hear it rustling through the trees, but you have no idea where it comes from or where it is headed next.

Let us face it, you have been born from above by my wind. That is pretty cool, huh? You are now a living spirit just like me. You have my nature. I created you in my image. You have absolute authority and control over your circumstances. Open your mouth and declare what you want. Call those things that be not as though they were. It is time that you renew your mind. Start hanging out with me more, and you will find life a lot easier. I will strengthen you, perfect you, and make you complete.

I will be responsible for making you who you ought to be. I want you to be encouraged and consoled and comforted. I want you to be of one mind with me. Then you will live in peace. Make me the source of everything that you do. Aim for perfection, and I will make you perfect. Reach for the Heavens, and you will see me. Seek my Kingdom and my way of doing things, and I will add everything that you need. You are my favored child. You will experience favor in every area of your life today. Expect it.

Remember that I love you,

Your Dad

I AM IN YOU

Dearly Beloved,

I am your Father and everything that you need is in me. Not only am I your Father, I am Almighty God. The God of the universe. The God who created the heavens and the earth. I also created you to rule the earth just like I do.

I want people to see me through you. You have been equipped with blessings that tumble out of the sky. Blessings bursting from the earth. Blessings that exceed the ancient mountains and surpass the delights of the eternal hills.

Now, with all that you have been blessed with, you need wisdom and very great insight. I will give you a breath of understanding as measureless as the sand on the seashore. All you must do is ask for it. I have already granted you the spirit of wisdom and revelation to know me better. When you know me better, you will know my thoughts. And when you know my thoughts, you will discover my ways just as Moses did.

You have found favor in my sight because you have chosen to become more deeply and intimately acquainted with me. When you give into me and come to terms with all my promises, everything will turn out fine. Come to me with your whole heart and I will rebuild your life.

Clean your house of everything evil. Relax your grip on your money and abandoned your gold-plated luxury. I am God Almighty, and I will be your treasure. More wealth than you can imagine. Then you will have delight in me. You can pray to me and I will hear you. I will make all your dreams come true.

Now remember that wisdom is a principal thing. Never walk away from her. She will guard your life. Real wisdom begins with a Holy life and it is characterized by getting along with others. It is gentle when reasonably overflowing with mercy and blessings. Not hot one day and cold the next. Not two-faced.

I want you to live wisely and humbly. Do not be confused. A wise person would know the difference. I want you to build a reputation for wisdom. It is the way you live, not the way you talk that counts. Keep in mind that mean-spirited ambition is not wisdom. Boasting that you are wise is not wisdom. Twisting the truth to make yourself sound wise is not wisdom. It is the furthest from the truth. True wisdom will take the focus off you and direct it towards me. So, do not waste your time on useless work—mere busy work—the barren pursuits of darkness. Expose these things for the sham they are. It is a scandal when people waste their lives on things they must do in the dark where no one else will see.

So, watch your step and use your head. Make the most of every chance you get. Everything you need is right here. Just ask for it.

I love you,

Dad

HOW YOU PRAY DOES MATTER

Dearly Beloved,

I want to remind you today that I am the God of Abraham, Isaac, and Jacob, and I am also your God. I am Jehovah, your covenant keeper. I have made many promises to you and I have not changed one of them. I want you to know how special you are to me. If you remain faithful and follow me, I will use you as a channel and allow all of my blessings to flow through you to the rest of the world.

You were chosen by me to be an instrument of my redemption. This covenant that you have available to you is not like a contract which always has an end date. It is a permanent arrangement. You can rest assure that everything I have written in my word is true. It is forever settled in heaven.

Now, it is very important that you are familiar with my promises. I will reveal them to you as you search the scriptures. When you find what you want, just ask for it. What you need and desire has already been prepared for you. Ask and it shall be given unto you. Seek and you shall find. Keep on knocking reverently and the door will be opened. I will personally open it for you. You do not have to bargain with me. I want you to be direct and ask me for what you need. You should be praying according to my word only. Do not be like the so-called prayer warriors who pray ignorance. They are full of formulas, programs, and advice. They peddle techniques to try to get what they want. Do not fall for that nonsense—not once. I am your Father and you are dealing directly with me through my son, Jesus Christ, the Anointed one and all of his anointings. When you come before me, do not turn your prayer into a theatrical production. I am not a God who sits in a box seat watching you make a regular show out of your prayers, hoping for stardom.

Here is what I want you to do. Find a quiet, secluded place so you will not be tempted to role play before me. As you sit there simply and honestly, your focus will shift from you to me. I will teach you my way so that you may walk and live in truth. I will direct and unite my heart to yours so that you will reverence me and honor my name. I will give you a lantern, a compass, and a map so that you can find your way to the sacred mountain, to the place where I reside. This is a place of worship. I will guide you until the end of time, detail by detail, so that you can tell your story. I will be a personal guide to you, directing you through unknown territory.

When you pray, I will be right there to show you what road to take, making sure you do not fall into a ditch. I will not leave you for a minute.

Now, for my covenant to be effective, you must get rid of unfair practices. Quit blaming victims, quit gossiping about other people's sins. If you are generous with the hungry and start giving yourself to the down and out, your life will begin to glow in the darkness. Your shadowed lives would be bathed in sunlight. I will always show you where to go. I will give you a full life in the emptiest of places: firm muscles, strong bones. You will be like a well-watered garden, a gurgling spring that never runs dry. You will be known as a child of the Most High. You have worked hard and deserve all that you have coming. Enjoy the blessing and revel in my goodness.

Remember, my covenant will endure forever.

I love you,

Dad

I HAVE DECIDED THE OUTCOME

Dearly Beloved,

I want to remind you today that you are my favored child. I love you with all that I am, and my favor surrounds you as a shield. I will bestow present grace and favor and future honor, splendor, and heavily bliss upon you. I will not withhold any good thing from you as you continue to walk upright. I have listened to and heeded to your call. From now on, people will call you blessed. You will see a manifestation of my goodness today.

When I called you out, I took one good look at you, and made you the most fortunate person on earth. What I have done and will do for you will never be forgotten. I have set you apart from all the others. My mercy flows through you wave after wave because you are in awe of me.

I will make up for the bad times with good times because you have seen enough evil to last a lifetime. I will give you double for your trouble. Instead of shame and dishonor, you will possess a double portion of prosperity in your land. And everlasting joy will be yours. I will look on you with favor and make you fruitful and multiply you.

I will establish my covenant with you before all the people

on earth. I will make your surroundings a place of peace. You will be able to go to sleep at night without fear. I will get rid of the old and bring in the new. I will give you my full attention, making sure that you prosper. And you will see growth in every area of your life. You will no longer be a slave to debt, despair, loneliness, sickness, lack, disease, hopelessness, or anything that keeps you in bondage. I brought you out to bring you into a land flowing with milk and honey. I have ripped off the harness of slavery so that you can move more freely.

I will set up my residence in your neighborhood. I will not avoid or shun you. I will stroll through the streets, and let everyone know that I am your God, your personal God, who rescued you and placed you on high, high above every negative occurrence in your life. I am the one who will promote you. Do not look for it from anyone else. I am the one who will have a last word over your life. I have decided the outcome.

Every good and perfect thing comes from me, and I decided long ago that I would share it with you. Remember that I am always with you, rooting for you, ready to give you a high five because you will reach a level of achievement that is worthy of acknowledgment.

You deserve a break today. Look for uncommon favor everywhere you go.

I love you,

Dad

KEEPING A FIRM GRIP

Dearly Beloved,

It is crucial that you keep a firm grip on what you have heard so that you do not drift off. You would do well to keep focusing on the voice behind these words. Every word you read today is a prophetic word that has been confirmed through the scriptures. It is the one light you have in a dark time as you wait for daybreak and the rising of the Morning Star in your heart.

The main thing to keep in mind is that no prophecy of scripture is a matter of private opinion. It is not something that has been concocted in the human heart. Prophecy resulted when my Holy Spirit prompted men and women to speak my word, so do not lose a minute in building on what you have been given, complementing your basic faith with good character, spiritual understanding, alert discipline, passionate patience, reverent wonder, warm friendliness, and generous love. Each dimension fitting into your development. With these qualities active and growing in your life, no grass will grow under your feet and no day will pass without its reward as you mature in your experience with your Master, Jesus. Without these qualities, you will not be able to see what is right before you.

Don't you know that your old sinful nature has been wiped off the books? Stop condemning yourself when you miss the mark. I have already prepared a way of escape. Everything that you have done wrong has been covered under the blood of Jesus. He personally took on the human condition, entered the disordered mess of struggling humanity to get it right once for all.

You will experience life on my terms now that I am alive and present within you. I would do the same thing that I did with Jesus, bringing you alive to myself. I live and I breathe in you. You have been delivered from your past life. You should no longer be absorbed in yourself. When you do that, you take the focus off me and what I am trying to do in your life. I want to bring you to a place of total trust in me.

There is no comparison between the present hard times and the coming good times. The difficult times that you are experiencing are simply birth pangs. The things that belong to you are arousing inside just like a woman who is about to give birth. Your body is yearning for full deliverance. That is why waiting will not diminish you any more than waiting diminishes a pregnant mother. You are enlarged in waiting. You may not see what is growing in you, but the longer you wait the larger those things become, and the more joyful your expectancy. Meanwhile, the moment you get tired of waiting, my spirit is right alongside helping you along.

If you do not know what to pray, I would do your praying for you. You can be sure that every detail of your life is worked into something good.

So, remember, keep a firm grip. You are about to give birth to the blessing.

I love you,

Dad

MY PROMISE

Dearly Beloved,

I want you to make a promise to me today. Promise me that you will spend every available minute acknowledging my presence. I am always available to you, but it is difficult for you to notice me because you are concerned with the cares of this world. Allow me to show up and show out in your life., and you could no longer deny me the privilege of taking care of you. Anticipate the best in every area of your life. Give yourself wholeheartedly holding nothing back.

I am with you. I am your one true God. I will never leave you or forsake you. I will not relax my hold on you. Come back to me and really mean it. Change your life, not your clothes. I am not concerned about your outward appearance as much as I am concerned about what's going on in your heart.

If you let me, I will create in you a clean heart and renew a right spirit within you. I will pour pure water over you and scrub you clean. I will remove the stony heart from your body and replace it with a heart that is God-willed, not self-willed. I will put my spirit in you and make it possible for you to do what I tell you. Then you will be able to live by my commands. I will multiply you and increase you so that you will no longer suffer the reproach and disgrace that is associated with the famine that is taking place in your land. I will lavish you with good things and bless the work of your hands. On top of that, I will bless you and multiply you as the stars in heaven. Your blessings will be full and robust, full of health and strength.

As you grow closer to me, you will be strong and do exploits. You will be capable of accomplishing extraordinary deeds. Everything you do will be noteworthy. I will bless you with an abundant increase of favor and make your name famous and distinguished. You will be a blessing dispensing good to others. You will be blessed beyond measure. This life is not for those who choose to stay where they are. You must make a decision to follow me with your whole heart. You must disregard, lose sight of, and forget yourself and your own interests. Cleave steadfastly to me, conform wholly to my example in living. I want your unwavering loyalty. You will not regret it. I promise.

Do not abandon what I have placed before you. I am sending you a gift today. Fear not, be glad and celebrate. Help is on the way. I will head off your enemies and dump them in a wasteland. There they will remain, never to be seen again. I will set you back on your heels in wonder. Never again will you have to worry. You will know without question that I am in the thick of life with you. There will be a great rescue, just as I said before the beginning of time.

When you acknowledge me, I will pour out my Spirit on you and show you signs, wonders, and miracles. You will never be the same.

Love always,

Dad

REJOICE AND BE GLAD

Dearly Beloved,

This is the day that I have made, and I want you to rejoice and be glad. You will experience gladness in a high degree today, as you begin to take your focus off yourself. I am taking you to a place in your thoughts that will enable you to engage wholly and deeply into what I am doing. I am in the driver's seat. Allow me to usher you into a place of total peace. We are going for a ride to a place where you will be submerged and overcome by my blessings.

Once we reach our destination, you will be overtaken by the forces of good and everything that comes with it. Here, you will take on the mind of Christ, totally trusting, relying, and depending completely on who you are in me, and more importantly, who I am to you. Without the mind of Christ, it would be impossible for you to comprehend what I want to do in your life today. But with the guidance of my Holy Spirit, you will have insight into my plans, thoughts, and actions.

I have taken you out of your mind and into mine, so that you will know with assurance that I am on your side. There is no need to fear anymore. I called you from the dark corners of the earth to keep a firm grip on you. I am your God and I will give you strength. I will help you and hold you steady. I have your back and you can always count on me. Everyone who had it in for you will end up out in the cold, real losers.

Those who worked against you will end up empty handed. When you look for your old adversaries—debt, despair, hopelessness, lack, fear, depression, and oppression—you will not find them. Not a trace of your old enemies, not even a memory. I am your God and I have a firm grip on you and I am not letting you go. I am telling you, do not panic. I am right here to help you.

I will come on the double as I listen to your prayers. I will not turn a deaf ear. I will stay with you. My love for you is loyal. I will bring you to a place that is well-watered. Look around, it will take your breath away. In this place, I will plant for you so that you will be like a tree replanted in Eden, bearing fresh fruit, never dropping a leaf, and always in blossom. You will be able to bring forth fruit in this season and everything that you choose to do will prosper as it comes to full maturity.

I created you to have the mind of Christ. It is not

something that you can put on or take off. From this day forward, you are in a perpetual state of mind control.

You will only think on those things that are excellent and worthy of praise. Keep putting into practice all you have learned and received from me today. We are at our destination. This is where you get off.

Have a Christ-centered day.

I love you,

Dad

THE HOLY ROAD

Dearly Beloved,

I want to take you on a journey today. My goal is to take you from a place of lack, to a place of more than enough. I am El Shaddai. I am the God of more than enough. Everything I do for you from now on will be over the top, a surplus, super abundant, overflowing, good measure, pressed down, shaken together, and running over.

There will be a highway called the Holy road. No one rude or rebellious is permitted on this road. It is exclusively for my chosen, my elect. You have been selected from a small group because of your desire to honor me. It is impossible for you to get lost on this road. Not even a fool can get lost. There will be no lions on this road to try to devour you, and no other dangerous wild animals, nothing or no one dangerous or threatening. Only the redeemed will walk on it. Only the people I have ransomed will be able to travel on this road and make their way to me. I want you to sing songs and hymns as you make your way home to Zion. There will be unfading hails of joy circling your head. And I will welcome you with open arms with gifts of joy and gladness.

Because you have relief from your enemies, your sorrow

will be turned to joy and your mourning somersaulted into a holiday of parties filled with fun and laughter. This Holy road would take you to a place of life everlasting. You would travel this road indefinitely, without intermission or interruption. I want you to travel this road with an outstretched neck. Even if it gets a little bumpy, remember the covenant that I have with you. I have given you a roadmap, which is the Word.

I have spelled out everything you need to know, even if I blindfolded you, it is important that you trust me. I would never lead you astray.

Now, place your feet on the light path. Take my hand and follow me. I am taking you to a place where you will be abundantly blessed and well-nourished. Do not look back like Lot's wife. You already know what is behind you: sickness, disease, lack, doubt, unbelief, poverty, confusion, and defeat. You are no longer a recipient of those things or anything that represents the curse. You are blessed and highly favored, and I want the world to know that you belong to me.

This Holy road will take you to a place on high, high above all the nations of the world. If you choose to respond to my voice all my blessings will come down on you and will be spread out before you. It is easier than you think. I have anointed your ears to hear what I am saying. You have no excuse. Your heart has already been prepared.

I love you with all that I am.

Your Dad

TIME IS ON YOUR SIDE

Dearly Beloved,

I know that you may not always believe that I love you and have the best for you, but I do. I realize that in your finite mind, you think that time is your enemy. In the heavenly realm, time has no beginning and no end. It just is. I know that you want what you want when you want it. Sometimes I wish I could give you what you want, but it is not always in your best interest for me to do that.

Do not look at waiting as a sign that I am not working on your behalf. Everything I do for you is in your best interest and those who are around you. I want you to wait on me. Time is your best friend right now. It is getting you ready and prepared to enter the land I promised you. A land flowing with milk and honey.

I do not want you to become disinterested in my plan for your life or to become a spiritual sluggard, but an imitator of those who walk by faith. It is important that you grow closer to me so that I can instruct you. You will need to learn my entire personality, so that you can have confidence in my power, wisdom, and goodness. You can do that by practicing patience and endurance. Nothing worth having will come easily.

I want you to appreciate all that I do for you. I want you to be able to say to the world, "Look at what the Lord has done." Waiting will build your faith muscles, so that you can endure any and everything that comes your way. I am building you up so that you can strengthen your brothers and sisters who have their hope and faith in me. So, do not be entangled with the things of this world.

Run with patient endurance and steady active persistence. I want you to look away from all that distracts you and look to Jesus who is the Author and Finisher of your faith. He will bring you to maturity and perfection. Keep your eyes on Him so that you will not grow weary or exhausted, losing heart and relaxing and fainting in your mind.

I strongly urge you to wait on me. Expect me, look for me and put all your hope in me. You will see a change, and your strength will be renewed. You will have power that will come from me. I will energize you when you get tired.

Remember, time in this life is on your side, so spread your wings and soar like an eagle. Try running and see that you will not get tired. Even when you walk, you will not lag.

Keep in mind that people will see you as blessed.

Sometimes they will even envy you because you stood up under temptation. You stood the test and I approved you. You will receive the victor's crown of life. You will be in a special class with those who chose to love me, rely on me, depend on me, and have confidence in me. You will be a recipient of my promises. So, go ahead and praise Me!

Know that I am a good God.

I love you.

Always,

Dad

WALK IN THE LIGHT

Dearly Beloved,

I want to remind you today that you are my child and I want the best for you. As my child, you will experience life beyond your wildest dreams. We are going to work together today to put your life in order.

First, I need your full attention. Nothing in the kingdom is by happenstance. Everything has been laid out for you. Every step you take today will be ordered by me. You are my sheep and I am your Shepherd. My voice is the only voice you should hear. Avoid the talk-show religion and the practiced confusion of the so-called experts. Those people are caught up in a lot of talk and they miss the whole point of walking by faith.

Guard the treasure that you have been given. Guard it with your life. Do not become partners with those who reject me. How can you make partnership out of right and wrong or light and darkness? That is not partnership. It is all out war. Can light be best friends with dark? Well, neither can you. Do you think that Jesus ever went strolling with the devil? Not a chance. Do trust and mistrust hold hands? I do not think so. Would you think of setting up pagan idols in my Holy temple? I hope not. You are my Holy temple.

Let me put it this way, I live in you and move in you. I am your God and you belong to me. There can be no harmony between me and Satan, and you have nothing in common as a believer with the unbeliever. I urge you not to team up with them. Be aware of the unrighteous. They will weaken your commitment, integrity, and your standards.

You should do everything in your power to avoid situations that would force you to divide your loyalties. Since you have discovered my light, there can be no fellowship or compromise with darkness. Do you see the difference? I do not want you to become part of something that reduces you to less than yourself. You cannot have it both ways, having a lavish and sumptuous meal with me one day and slumming with the demons the next. I will not allow it. Do not think that you can get away with it. I want nothing less than all of you. All or nothing. There is no need for you to be ignorant of these matters anymore. You are no longer a mere human.

Set yourself to pursue righteousness and a godly life. A life of wonder, faith, love, steadiness, and courtesy. Run hard and fast in the faith. Seize the eternal life that you were called to--the life you so fervently embrace in the presence of so many witnesses.

I am charging you not to give in an inch. I am commanding you to follow these instructions to the letter and do not slack off. Continue to be rich in helping others, even if they are not of the household of faith. Be extravagantly generous, this way you will build a treasure that will last forever. Do not be deceived. Follow the light and it will lead you to true riches. I made a promise to you that I would never leave you or forsake you.

Look out! Your wildest dreams are about to come true.

I love you.

Dad

COME TO ME

Dearly Beloved,

    I want you to run, not walk into my arms today. My arms are open wide waiting for you to take refuge in me. In my arms, you will experience a peace that surpasses all understanding. I am your rock and I want you to take refuge in me. In my arms, I will keep you safe. I am reaching for you so that I can protect you. My way is perfect, and I will be a shield to you when you trust me. Everyone who runs towards me will make it. There are no losers in this race. Run, do not walk!

    I am waiting for you. I long to pick you up and place you on solid ground. I will arm you with strength and make your way perfect. I am the God who will arm you, then aim you in the right direction. I will clear the ground under you and make sure your footing is firm. In my arms, you will be close to my face. Your ears will be close to my mouth. Even in a small whisper, you will be able to hear me. When you are close to my face, you will experience an intimacy that will bring us closer. You do not have to worry about a thing. I have taken care of everything for you.

Use your imagination. I gave it to you. Envision yourself as a child wrapped in my arms. I will not let anything harm you. I am your protector. I will keep you safe, forever. All your enemies have to bow down to me. Confusion, sickness, lack, uncertainty, debt, distress, poverty, you name it, it must bow down to the name of Jesus. Declare that those things are under your feet. Sit alongside me here on my throne. I have taken you from my lap to a seat that I have prepared for you.

You have gone from my arms to my face and now you are seated with Christ in the heavenly realm. Now you can rule over your life. I created you just like me.

Your circumstances will no longer rule you. You can use your mouth to change or rearrange things. Call out what you want, and I will be right there to watch it happen. Even though your tongue may be small, it is very powerful. Begin to use it as a weapon of faith.

Remember that your faith does not stand in the wisdom of men but in my power. So, go ahead and call those things that be not as though they were. If you need help while you're in my arms seeking my face, I will turn my mouth to your ear, and I will gently tell you what to say. Now, do you see the benefit of coming into my arms? Selah!

My arms are not too short to reach for you.

I love you,

Daddy

WATCH YOUR MOUTH

Dearly Beloved,

Everywhere you go today, and everything you do, I want you to be mindful of what is coming out of your mouth. I am very concerned that you do not realize how powerful your words are. Remember, you are created in my image and in my likeness. You are a speaking spirit. I created the heavens and the earth by speaking them into existence. You can create your heaven and your earth by what you say.

In the beginning I prepared, formed, and fashioned exactly what I wanted to manifest. When I wanted light, I said it and it was so. It was good, suitable, and pleasant. I decided to call light day and the darkness night, and it was so. I spoke what I wanted to see, watched it happen and then approved it, and so can you.

I made you holy, blameless, righteous, and justified, with my words. I said it was so, and that is who you are. No matter who you think you are, you are perfect because I call you perfect. I shaped you first inside and then out. I know exactly how you are made. I sculpted you from nothing to something. I spoke who you are into existence. You are fearfully and wonderfully made by my words. I called

Abraham the father of many Nations and many, many years later, you are his seed and an heir according to My promise. Don't you see how powerful your words are? They can affect your world and your children and your children's children.

When you speak my words, they will be more powerful than a two-edged sword. When you use your mouth for evil, evil will happen. When you use your mouth for good, good will happen. Your tongue is like the pen of a ready writer, spilling beauty and goodness into the earth.

Your deliverance is in your mouth. I am your deliverer and when you agree with me, you will see a manifestation of what you need. You own your lips and you will triumph with your tongue. The mouth of the righteous, that is you, utters wisdom and his tongue speaks what is just. Use your mouth to speak of righteousness and begin to praise me all day long. I am the Spirit of the Lord who is speaking through you. Let my words be on your tongue. Do not allow your words to be reckless. Let them bring healing as a tree of life. Let your lips drop sweetness as the honeycomb. Not only do I want you to keep your mind on whatever is true and honorable and right and pure and lovely and admirable, I want your words to reflect those things that I mentioned above.

So, if you are serious about living a life of peace and

prosperity, pursue and speak those things that Christ presides over. He is the High Priest of your profession. His job is to tell me what you want. He will only speak to me what you have spoken that agrees with my word. He is my messenger. I appointed him just for you. I entrusted him with your words.

So, remember to speak the word only today and every day. Use your words to create your world just like I created mine. You will have whatsoever you say. You will see victory in your trials. I agree with you.

Have a Christ-centered day.

I love you.

Dad

PRAISE IS YOUR BREAKTHROUGH

Dearly Beloved,

I do not want you to forget how important it is to praise. Praise would allow me to send a spiritual earthquake your way--a tsunami that will wash away everything that represents evil in your life. In the time of trials, you will get the victory by praising your Lord and Savior, Jesus Christ. Praise will confuse the enemy and make him turn the other way. Praise indicates that you have a confident expectation that your needs are met. It will allow you to put doubt and unbelief on the shelf and leave them there.

You seem to forget that I have done many things for you. I have backed up my promises with the authority of my name. I am your praise and I am your God. Reverently respect me, acknowledge me, and hold tight to me. Begin to offer a sacrifice of praise today. This way you will have a richer harvest. Praise will put you on the right track and allow me to deliver your enemies into your hands. From now on, your assignment is to praise me on a regular basis.

I hold strength and power in the palm of my hand to build you up. Everything on earth and in heaven belongs to me. When you offer a praise, you can quickly get those things into your hands. Riches and glory come from me, but I am more than capable of sharing them with you. Your praise brings you closer to me and brings me closer to you. We will be bound by mutual interest and loyalties.

The forces of evil have no power over you and your praise will keep you from falling prey to the enemy's devices. Satan's desire is to trip you up and sift you as wheat. He will throw multiple distractions, trials, and ideas at you. Praise will shield you from the fiery darts of the devil. Those darts contain furious suggestions of evil and enticement to sin. They contain blasphemous thoughts, unbelief, sudden temptation to do wrong or thoughts that would wound and torment the soul. Remember, your praise will shut the devil up. He will have no say in your life. He will flee from you and he will think twice about coming back.

Praise will remind you of how good I am and how much I want to move on your behalf. I will inhabit the atmosphere of praise and you will see a clear manifestation of my blessings and grace.

Praise is useful and favorable for you. It will remind you of my greatness and that my power and presence are in your life. Glorify me with thanksgiving. Celebrate my goodness and my grace. Praise me with all your heart and all your soul. I created the heavens and the earth and all that comes with it. I am worthy to be praised.

Sing, dance, shout, jump for joy! Clap your hands and it will result in all my power, love, and grace for you. Just keep on praising. Take your mind off your problems and shortcomings. It will help you to focus on me. Praise would cause you to consider and appreciate my character. Praise will lift your perspective from the earthly to the heavenly. Praise will prepare your heart to receive my love and the power that comes from the Holy Spirit. I created this day just for you. Look for me in your praise.

I love you,

Dad

BONUS CONTENT

MY GRACE IS SUFFICIENT

Dearly Beloved,

I am the God of all Grace. I am the one who imparts all blessings and favor upon you. I am the one true God that has called you into my eternal glory in Christ Jesus. I have made you complete, and you are everything you need to be. I have established and grounded you. Trust me. You are secure and I have already made you strong. I have created you to be firm in the faith. You are rooted, immovable, and determined. I want you to remember that from the very beginning, you were saved by grace through faith.

I gave you this wonderful gift to govern your entire life by my divine power that is always working in you. Just allow it to permeate your mind, your heart, and your emotions. I have my eyes on you. I love you so much, I have you engraved in the palm of my hand. I am determined by the work of my Holy Spirit to keep you through the sacrifice of your Master Jesus.

You are so fortunate to have me as your Father. Meditate on my love for you which is shed abroad in your heart. Because of my grace I am giving you a brand-new life and you have everything to live for, including a future in Heaven.

Let me remind you that your future in Heaven starts now. The day is coming when you will experience it all. Allow my grace to work it out for you. I love you so much that I raised Jesus from the dead. Ask your neighbors if their God can do that.

Your life is a journey that you must travel with a deep consciousness of my grace. It was by My grace that you were able to get out of that dead and empty-headed life that you grew up in. It was by my grace that Jesus died like an unblemished sacrificial lamb; to keep you in a life full of Mercy. My mercies are new every day and they endure forever. You can always count on me. I promise you I would never leave you or forsake you. It is my grace that will cause you to believe that I would never let you down. I would never walk off and leave you. I will not relax my hold on you.

I want to remind you of how good you have it. Remember that old plan that I had with your ancestors? No matter how many sacrifices were offered year after year they never added up to a complete solution. The old plan which is the law was only a hint of the good things in the new plan of Grace. The law came by Moses, but Grace and Truth came by Jesus. All the law did was to heighten their awareness of sin and guilt. You do not have to worry about living under the law; you have already been redeemed by my grace. Embrace grace! The law will only keep you in bondage locked up like a slave trying to work yourself out of prison. You are free and who the Son sets free is free indeed. You are made fit because of the sacrifice of Jesus. The doors have been opened and you can come free from the bars of imprisonment. No more works! It is time to live by my grace!

Love always,

Dad

YOUR SLATE HAS BEEN WIPED CLEAN

Dearest Beloved,

This is the first day of the rest of your life. What are you going to do with it? Your slate has been wiped clean. I do not remember your unrighteous deeds. I have crowned you with righteousness and glory and honor. I said I would bless you and increase you. What are you going to do with that?

I made you holy and blameless. I said I would supply all your needs according to my riches in glory. What are you expecting on your new day with new mercies? You can decide your day today. Will you believe my report or the report of your enemy who desires to sift you as wheat? Don't you know that I prayed that your faith would not fail?

I need you to strengthen your brothers and sisters. I need you to help me expand the Kingdom. I need you to reintroduce Jesus. I want you to showcase my Son. I want my Glory to shine on you. You are blessed, empowered to prosper in every area of your life.

Whether you believe it or not, there is an abundant supply of everything you need. I provided it for you before the foundation of the world. You can access it by faith. You now have the keys to the Kingdom. Use them!

My job is to give; yours is to receive. My grace is sufficient for you. You have all the favor you need to do whatever you need, whenever you need it. I have looked on you with favor and made you fruitful so that you will multiply. I will make your name great. My divine order has put you in the front of the line. Nothing has changed because you favor my righteous cause.

I want you to live freely and expansively. I will make you shine. I am transforming you right now! You will go from glory to glory to glory. Relax and enjoy the ride. I am in the driver's seat now! People will see more of me.

Thank you for acknowledging me in all your ways. Thank you for trusting me with all your heart. Thank you for allowing me to use you. You have been anointed. Use the power I have bestowed upon you. Never – I say it emphatically – never let your heart be troubled again. I got this! Remember, I am your personal God. I will never leave you or forsake you. You will never be ashamed. You have the victory!

This is my decree for you today that "Things are going to happen so fast your head will swim, one thing fast on the heels of the other. You will not be able to keep up. Everything will be happening at once—and everywhere you look, blessings! Blessings like wine pouring off the mountains and hills."

I will make everything right again for you. You have waited long enough.

Love,

Dad

MY LOVE FOR YOU IS INEXHAUSTIBLE

Dearly Beloved,

I want you to look at your big brother Jesus today. He is a centerpiece of everything that you believe. He is the Author and Finisher of your faith. He is faithful and everything that I have given him. Now Moses was faithful, but Jesus gets far more honor. Look at it this way, a builder is more valuable than a building any day. Every house has a builder but, the Builder (that is Jesus) is behind it all. Moses did a good job in my house, but it was all about serving work. Getting things ready for what was to come. Christ, as my Son, oversees the house.

There are so many things that are going on in the world right now. I do not want you to jump to any conclusions that we are not on the job. Instead, be glad that you are in the very thick of what Christ experienced. You are going through a spiritual refining process, but glory is just around the corner.

I declare today that you will be a recipient of my extravagant blessings. I have made you whole, ready and meet for my use. This time that you have been spending with me has prepared you and made you available for my service. You have been equipped with power from on high. I want you to keep this in mind: as Jesus is so are you in this world. Grace and peace have been bestowed upon you. Because of His sacrifice, and the blood that was poured out on the altar of the Cross, you are free of penalties and punishments chalked up by all your misdeeds. And not just barely free either, you are abundantly free!

It is in Christ that you will find out who you are and what your purpose is in this life. Long before you heard of him and got your hopes up, he had his eye on you. You were chosen to partake in the glorious long-range plans that we took delight in making on your behalf. The overall purpose for your life is working out. You have been signed, sealed, and delivered.

I am an honorable God, and these words I have spoken to you today, I guarantee forever. I will do exactly as I have promised. My reputation will be confirmed. People will know that I am your God. Your house will remain rock solid under my watchful presence. Even your family will be blessed. Even though they are not innocent, because of the cleanness of your hands, they will be delivered.

Continue to seek my face and pray daily. Your effectual

fervent prayer will avail much. I will turn my ears your way because your prayer is your last and only hope. When you pray, the little that you have will increase greatly. Everything I do for you will flourish under my care and will result in supernatural blessings. Remain steadfast, unmovable, always abounding in things that concern the kingdom. You are about to step into the other side.

Remember my love for you is immeasurable and inexhaustible.

Love,

Dad

YOUR FUTURE IS AS BRIGHT AS YOUR FAITH

Dearly Beloved,

I want you to know today that I love you so very much. Everything does not always turn out the way you want it to turn out, but I still want you to continue to trust me with your whole heart. Do not try to figure out everything on your own. Listen for my voice in all that you do and everywhere that you go today. I am the one who will keep you on track.

I know that you are very disappointed today, but nothing has changed. I love you with an everlasting love and I have compassion for you. I do not want you to feel abandoned. I have not forgotten the Covenant that I have with you and the ones that you love. I love them too. There are circumstances that happen in this life that will go against everything that you believe in the natural, but I want to encourage you to look through your spiritual eyes and you will know with assurance that everything will be alright.

Remember that all things work together for good because you are the called and my purpose will be fulfilled in you. That, what seems like the end for others is the beginning for them. You can be sure that every detail is worked out for something good.

I knew what I was doing from the very beginning. I decided from the outset to shape the lives of those who belong to me. You belong to me. I have placed you on solid ground. I have established you and will stay with you to the end, gloriously completing what I have begun in you. I have raised you to a Heavenly dignity because I love you. Never lose sight of that.

You have everything that you need to make it beyond this point. I call you blessed, happy, fortunate, spiritually prosperous and to be envied because you will endure without wavering during this time of tribulation. This experience will test your endurance, patience, and faith. I have confidence in you that you will make it because I will not relax my hold on you, assuredly not! You may not see things clearly now--you are squinting in the fog, peering through a mist--but it will not be long before the weather clears, and the sun will shine bright. You will see as clearly as I see. You will experience reality face-to-face. Look for perfection because it is coming.

Continue to have a joyful and confident expectation of eternal salvation. Remain hopeful and most of all love extravagantly. There are people all around you that need you. Give love and it will be given back to you. Always keep in mind that you reap what you sow. Be of good cheer when adversity strikes. Your future is as bright as your faith.

I was speaking to you today so that you will be unshakably assured and deeply at peace. I will always be with you. Your joy will be like a river overflowing its banks!

Love always,

Dad

ACKNOWLEDGMENTS

I'd like to thank my graphic designer and web developer Michelle 'Misha' Mace with Norwest Designs her wisdom, support and guidance on this project has been invaluable. I would not have been able to complete it without her. www.norwestdesigns.com

If you would like more information, please contact:

Deborah L. Clark

PO Box 3821 Alexandria, Va. 22304

(703) 879-8439

dclark@lettersfromalmightygod.com

Letters From Almighty God - Learn More at: www.lettersfromalmightygod.com
#lettersfromalmightygod

Made in United States
North Haven, CT
23 April 2025

68247671R00039